Über Bee German

About Bee German

> Hallo! Ich heiße Oskar. Du kannst mich anmalen. Benutze die Farben gelb, schwarz, blau und pink. Viel Spaß!
>
> Hello! My name is Oskar. You can colour me in. Use the colours yellow, black, blue and pink. Have fun!

Bee German has been created by Madeleine, an experienced German tutor from Germany. She has worked in various settings, such as language schools and preschools, across the UK, Ireland and Germany. Because of the lack of German learning resources for children, Madeleine created an online learning platform and this marvellous workbook.
Visit www.beegerman.com for more information.

INHALT

Contents

VORWORT

Foreword

Children are interested in other languages and enjoy learning about other cultures and people. Therefore, a fun learning environment with interesting materials and activities is the key to a successful language learning experience. This workbook, my website beegerman.com and my videos will provide you with various materials, ideas and much inspiration to guarantee that your children/students improve their German language skills.

Bee German Volume 1 is suitable for absolute beginners and advanced students from the reading age upwards. The exercises and corresponding pictures are designed to increase your children/students' vocabulary knowledge. Furthermore, the first sentence patterns and important grammatical aspects are introduced. By the end of this book, your child/student will have a language foundation with enough vocabulary to have basic conversations.

Teaching and learning a foreign language is like building a house. You need to have a solid foundation to build sturdy walls and a resilient roof. Similarly, every foreign language journey starts with a good foundation that consists of basic vocabulary, grammar and sentences. Just as a house must withstand thunderstorms, wind, the sun and heavy rain, knowing a foreign language can make children stronger and increase their confidence in every aspect of life.

Tips and tricks for parents and teachers

- Use our **online course** in conjunction with this book! Check out: **www.beegerman.com** or our YouTube channel.
- Ensure that language learning is fun for your students/children. In this sense, 'play' should be an important part of your language sessions. Therefore, this workbook must be considered as an addition to songs, conversations and games.
- Too much pressure and too many expectations could reduce your children/students' interest. Focus on the positives and the achievements of your children/students.
- Collaboration plays an important part in language learning. An encouraging relationship between students and teacher or children and parent is especially important.
- Always remember: mistakes are a natural part of the language learning process. Keep your children/students motivated by giving positive encouragement.
- Repetition and revision are essential factors in language learning. New vocabulary and grammatical structures should be repeated briefly in every lesson.

BeeGerman.com

AKTIVITÄTEN

Activities

- **Online course:** Use our online course in conjunction with this workbook. Check out: www.beegerman.com.

- **Colourful, eye-catching displays:** Engaging displays can help children to memorise new vocabulary and grammatical structures. You can buy posters online or make your own. However, it is also important that children create their own displays. Provide the equipment and your knowledge and let your students work on their own posters.

- **Write your own lyrics:** You don't have to be a musician to co-write simple but effective lyrics with your students. You could start a lesson with a song that repeats words and basic German sentences from previous lessons.

- **Songs and rhymes:** If you are not too keen on writing your own songs, you could use YouTube as it is a great resource for German songs for children. New language patterns and vocabulary can be learned more easily with songs and rhymes.

- **Flashcards:** Flashcards are especially good for revising vocabulary in a fun way. They can also be used to play one of my favourite games called 'Memory', for which you simply need to use two sets of flashcards. This matching game and other memory and guessing games enable children to learn new vocabulary and sentences in an enjoyable way. As we all know, play is extremely important as it develops children's creativity and supports their brain development.

- **Drama activities:** Even if your students have limited language knowledge, drama activities can be especially useful. In my language lessons, my students like to pretend to go to a market to shop for vegetables and fruits. The contextual meaning helps the children to remember words and phrases. Furthermore, it increases students' motivation and interest in the German culture.

- **Guess the noun:** Another very popular game is 'Draw the noun', which is especially useful for reviewing vocabulary in a fun way. You could use flashcards as prompts; however, your students are not allowed to draw the image that is displayed on the flashcard. You could even ask your students to use full sentences, such as 'Das ist ein Buch' instead of 'Buch' or 'das Buch'.

- **German folder:** Your students should have a folder for collecting worksheets, pictures and flashcards. It is a great way of gathering language knowledge and repeating words and structures that have already been learned.

- **Bee German website and YouTube channel:** Are you looking for more ideas? Check out our website www.beegerman.com and our YouTube channel, which has many videos, songs and fun ideas for activities.

BeeGerman.com

Lese und Lerne

Hallo, wie geht es dir?
Hello, how are you?

Guten Morgen
Good morning

Gute Nacht
Good night

Wichtige Wörter und Sätze

Important words and sentences

Bitte
Please

Danke
Thank you

Guten Tag
Good day

Mir geht es schlecht.
I'm unwell.

Guten Abend Good evening

Wie heißt du?
What's your name?

Tschüss/ Auf Wiedersehen
Bye/ Goodbye

Mir geht es gut, danke.
I'm fine, thank you.

Mein Name ist...
Ich heiße...
My name is...

A. Male passende Bilder.
Draw matching pictures.

Guten Morgen
Good morning

Guten Tag
Good day

Guten Abend
Good evening

Gute Nacht
Goodnight

B. Verbinde die deutschen Wörter mit den englischen Wörtern.
Match the German words with the English words.

Guten Tag   Good morning

Hallo   Good night

Bitte   Hello

Guten Morgen   Bye

Guten Abend   Thank you

Auf Wiedersehen   Good day

Tschüss   Please

Danke   Good evening

Gute Nacht   Goodbye

Guten Tag!

Wie geht's?

BeeGerman.com

C. Verbinde die Sätze.
Match the sentences.

1. Wie geht es dir?   My name is...

2. Mir geht es gut, danke.   What's your name?

3. Wie heißt du?   I'm fine, thank you.

4. Mein Name ist...   How are you?

5. Mir geht es schlecht.   My name is...

6. Ich heiße...   I'm unwell.

Now you can have your first conversation in German!

SCHREIBEN

WRITING

D. Kopiere die Wörter, Sätze und Fragen.
Copy the words, sentences and questions.

1. Wie geht es dir?
   How are you?

   WIE GEHT ES DIR?
   _____

2. Tschüss!
   Bye!

   Tschüss
   _____

3. Ich heiße...
   My name is...

   Ich heiße
   _____

4. Danke!
   Thank you!

   Danke
   _____

5. Guten Tag!
   Good day!

   Guten Tag
   _____

6. Hallo!
   Hello!

   Hallo
   _____

DAS BIN ICH!

THAT'S ME!

Guten Tag! Mein Name ist Lena. Wie heißt du? Wie geht es dir?
Good day! My name is Lena. What's your name? How are you?

Hallo! Ich heiße Markus. Mir geht es gut, danke. Wie geht es dir?
Hello! My name is Markus. I'm well, thank you. How are you?

E. Beantworte die Fragen.
Answer the questions.

1. Wie geht es dir? Mir geht es _gut_____, danke.

2. Wie heißt du? Ich heiße _Amelie_____.

   Mein Name ist _Amelie_____.

F. Male dein Gesicht. Was kannst du schon sagen?
Draw your face. What can you say already?

#Kawaii

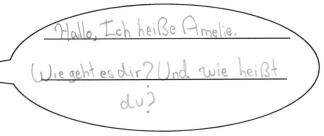

Hallo, Ich heiße Amelie.
Wie geht es dir? Und wie heißt du?

BeeGerman.com

NAMEN

NAMES

G. Schreibe Sätze. Benutze „Mein Name ist…" oder „Ich heiße…".
Write sentences. Use 'Mein Name ist…' or 'Ich heiße…'.

1. Ben

Mein Name ist
_____BEN_____

2. Sabrina

Ich heiße
_____Sabrina_____

3. Tom

_Ich heiße Tom_____

4. Anja

_Ich heiße Anja_____

5. Oskar

_Ich heiße Oskar_____

Lese und Lerne

Read and learn

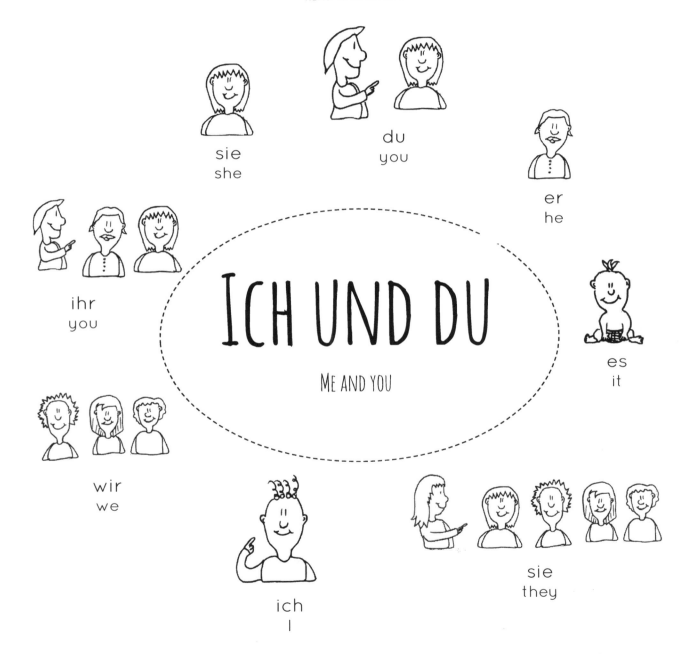

sie
she

du
you

er
he

ihr
you

Ich und du

Me and you

es
it

wir
we

ich
I

sie
they

12

BeeGerman.com

A. Verbinde die deutschen Wörter mit den englischen Wörtern.
Match the German words with the English words.

ich

du

er

sie

es

sie

ihr

wir

he

I

it

you

she

we

you

they

ZAHLEN

1	-	eins
2	-	zwei
3	-	drei
4	-	vier
5	-	fünf
6	-	sechs
7	-	sieben
8	-	acht
9	-	neun
10	-	zehn

A. Zähle die Bären und Vögel. Schreibe die Zahl in den Kreis.
Count the bears and birds. Write the number in the circle.

1

FÜNF

Bären
bears

2

drei

Vögel
birds

3

vier

Bären
bears

4
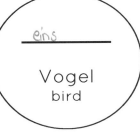

eins

Vogel
bird

14

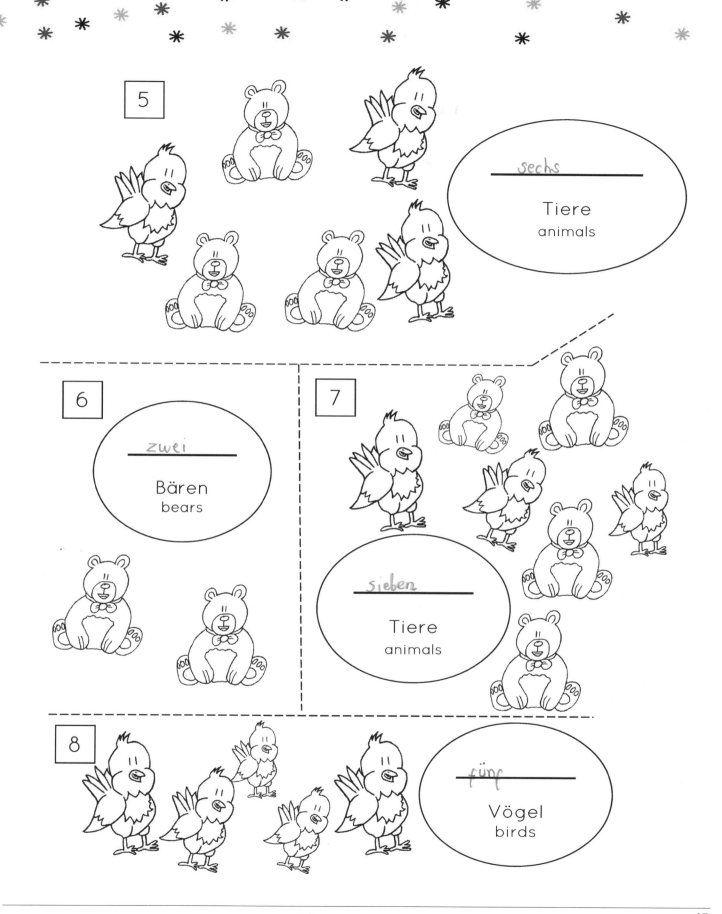

5

sechs

Tiere
animals

6

zwei

Bären
bears

7

sieben

Tiere
animals

8

fünf

Vögel
birds

BeeGerman.com

B. Schreibe die Zahl in den Kasten.
Write the number in the box.

1   EINS _____

3   drei _____

5   fünf _____

6   sechs _____

10   zehn _____

2   zwei _____

UMLAUTE
UMLAUTS
Ä, Ö, Ü

ZAHLENSALAT

NUMBER SALAD

C. Finde die unteren Zahlen im Gitter.
Find the numbers below in the grid.

- eins 1 ✓	- fünf 5 ✓	- neun 9 ✓
- zwei 2 ✓	- sechs 6 ✓	- zehn 10 ✓
- drei 3 ✓	- sieben 7 ✓	
- vier 4 ✓	- acht 8 ✓	

E	A	B	C	N	I	V	I	E	R	I
I	T	Y	K	Z	K	G	P	I	G	S
N	C	Z	Ü	E	A	N	E	U	N	I
S	S	A	C	H	T	B	L	E	F	E
F	D	Ä	K	N	M	D	C	H	D	B
Y	H	H	I	W	U	R	J	N	X	E
M	M	G	W	A	C	E	T	F	N	N
R	O	B	Z	W	E	I	U	Ü	E	R
F	K	V	H	F	K	R	K	N	U	X
B	O	I	S	S	J	O	I	F	F	I
S	E	C	H	S	H	M	P	N	F	R

zwei

WIE ALT BIST DU?

How old are you?

D. Wie alt sind die Kinder? Schreibe Sätze.
How old are the children? Write sentences.

1. | Tom, 9 Jahre | TOM IST NEUN JAHRE ALT.
Tom is nine years old.

2. | Katrin, 8 Jahre | Katrin ist acht jahre alt

3. | Anton, 10 Jahre | Anton ist zehn jahre alt

4.  | Petra, 6 Jahre | Petra ist sechs jahre alt

5.  | Annika, 7 Jahre | Annika ist sieben jahre alt

Und du? Wie alt bist du? Du kannst auch dein Gesicht malen!
And you? How old are you? You can also draw your face!

6.

Ich bin  elf jahre alt .

BeeGerman.com

Früchte und Gemüse

Fruits and vegetables

A. Lese und male die Früchte und das Gemüse an. Schreibe die richtige Zahl in den Kreis.
Read and colour in the fruits and vegetables. Write the correct number in the circle.

1. Nummer eins: Die Trauben sind lila. Number one: the grapes are purple.
2. Nummer zwei: Die Zitrone ist gelb. Number two: the lemon is yellow.
3. Nummer drei: Die Orange ist orange. Number three: the orange is orange.
4. Nummer vier: Die Karotte ist orange. Number four: the carrot is orange.
5. Nummer fünf: Die Paprika ist gelb. Number five: the pepper is yellow.
6. Nummer sechs: Die Tomate ist rot. Number six: the tomato is red.
7. Nummer sieben: Die Gurke ist grün. Number seven: the cucumber is green.
8. Nummer acht: Der Apfel ist rot. Number eight: the apple is red.
9. Nummer neun: Die Banane ist gelb. Number nine: the banana is yellow.
10. Nummer zehn: Die Birne ist grün. Number ten: the pear is green.

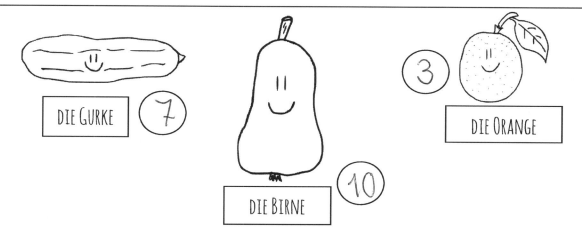

DIE GURKE 7

DIE BIRNE 10

3 DIE ORANGE

BeeGerman.com

Artikel

DER	-	THE (MASCULINE)
DIE	-	THE (FEMININE)
DAS	-	THE (NEUTER)

4

DIE KAROTTE

1

DIE TRAUBEN

5

DIE PAPRIKA

2

DIE ZITRONE

9

DIE BANANE

6

DIE TOMATE

8

DER APFEL

BeeGerman.com

FARBEN

Colours

B. Male die Ballons in der richtigen Farbe an.
Colour the balloons in the correct colour.

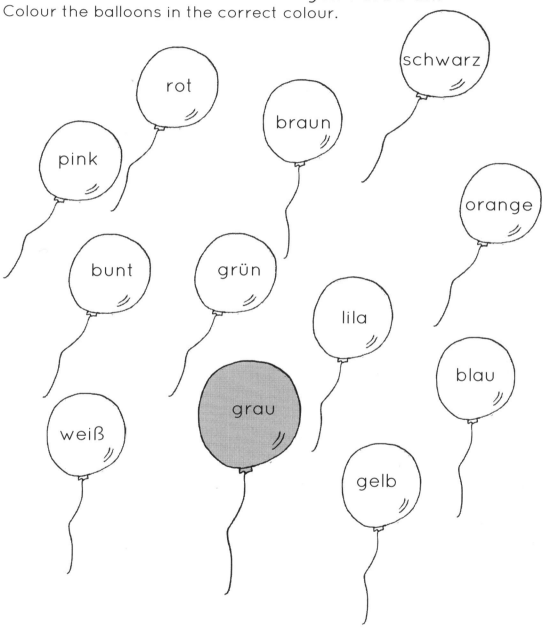

ICH MAG...

I LIKE...

C. Welche Früchte und welches Gemüse magst du/ magst du nicht?

Which fruits and which vegetables do you like/ do you not like?

1. Magst du Birnen?
   Do you like pears?

Ja, ich mag Birnen. / Nein, ich mag <u>keine</u> Birnen.
Yes, I like pears. / No, I don't like pears.

2. Magst du Äpfel?
   Do you like apples?

_____

3. Magst du Karotten?
   Do you like carrots?

_____

4. Magst du Tomaten?
   Do you like tomatoes?

_____

5. Magst du Bananen?
   Do you like bananas?

_____

6. Magst du Zitronen?
   Do you like lemons?

_____

7. Magst du Orangen?
   Do you like oranges?

_____

WOCHENTAGE

DAYS OF THE WEEK

A. Finde die Wochentage im Gitter. Dann schreibe die Wochentage in der richtigen Reihenfolge auf.
Find the days of the week in the grid. Then write the days of the week in the correct order.

- Montag	- Freitag	- Samstag	- Dienstag
- Mittwoch	- Sonntag	- Donnerstag	

MONTAG,_____

M	O	N	T	A	G	C	M	O	F	S
Z	X	P	Q	W	U	D	J	N	R	O
C	T	B	N	I	N	I	T	B	E	N
D	I	E	N	S	T	A	G	W	I	N
M	I	T	T	W	O	C	H	B	T	T
B	O	A	S	S	J	S	I	D	A	A
B	D	G	S	A	M	S	T	A	G	G
Y	B	P	S	F	C	A	N	M	M	R
D	O	N	N	E	R	S	T	A	G	I

BeeGerman.com

Lese und Lerne

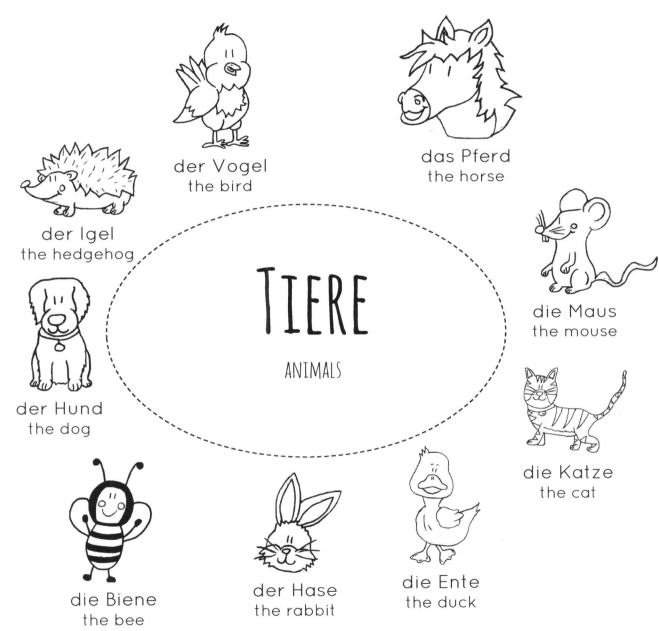

der Vogel
the bird

das Pferd
the horse

der Igel
the hedgehog

Tiere

ANIMALS

die Maus
the mouse

der Hund
the dog

die Katze
the cat

die Biene
the bee

der Hase
the rabbit

die Ente
the duck

TIERE

ANIMALS

A. Schreibe die passende Zahl in den Kreis.
Write the correct number in the circle.

1. der Hund

2. der Vogel

3. die Katze

4. der Hase

5. das Pferd

6. die Biene

7. der Igel

8. die Maus

9. die Ente

ARTIKEL		
THE	–	A
DER	–	EIN
DIE	–	EINE
DAS	–	EIN

B. Vervollständige die Sätze. Benutze „ein" oder „eine".
Complete the sentences. Use 'a'.

1. Das ist _____ EINE Katze.

This is a cat.

2. Das ist _____

3. Das ist _____

4. Das ist _____

5. Das ist _____

6. Das ist _____

7. Das ist _____

8. Das ist _____

9. Das ist _____

BeeGerman.com

Lese und Lerne

die Tochter/ die Schwester
the daughter/ the sister

der Onkel
the uncle

die Oma
the grandmother

der Cousin
the cousin

FAMILIE

FAMILY

die Tante
the aunt

der Sohn/ der Bruder
the son/ the brother

der Opa
the grandfather

der Vater
the father

die Mutter
the mother

DIE FAMILIE

THE FAMILY

A. Wer ist wer? Setze die Wörter ein.
Who is who? Fill in the words.

| Vater | Bruder/ Sohn | Tante | Opa |
| Mutter | Schwester/ Tochter | Onkel | Cousin |

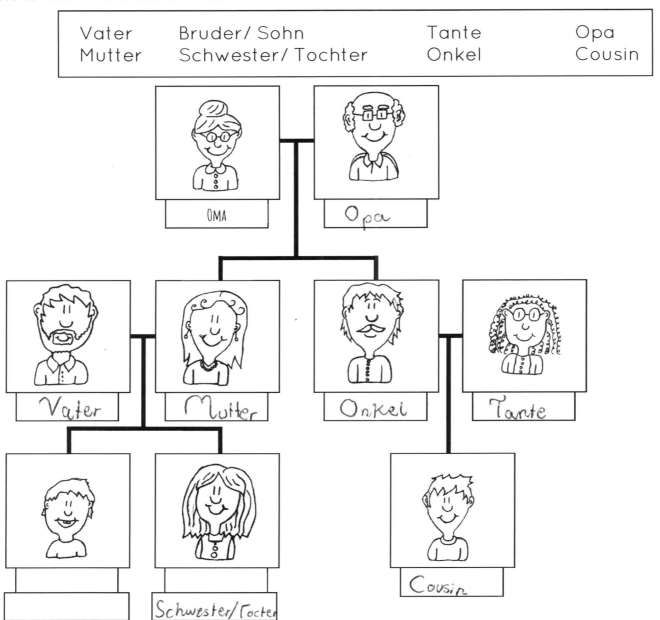

BeeGerman.com

LESE UND LERNE

Read and learn

der Regen
the rain

der Wind
the wind

der Schnee
the snow

die Wolke
the cloud

WETTER

WEATHER

das Gewitter
the thunderstorm

die Sonne
the sun

DAS WETTER

THE WEATHER

A. Verbinde die Wörter mit den Bildern und Sätzen.
Match the words with the pictures and sentences.

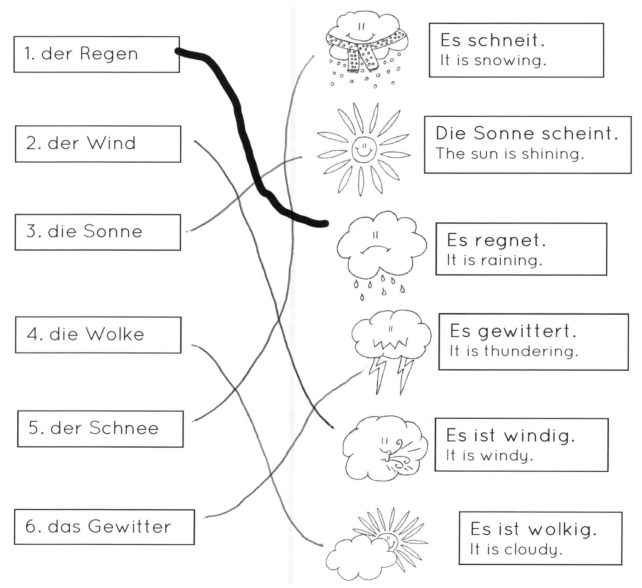

1. der Regen

2. der Wind

3. die Sonne

4. die Wolke

5. der Schnee

6. das Gewitter

Es schneit.
It is snowing.

Die Sonne scheint.
The sun is shining.

Es regnet.
It is raining.

Es gewittert.
It is thundering.

Es ist windig.
It is windy.

Es ist wolkig.
It is cloudy.

BeeGerman.com

DEUTSCHLANDKARTE

Map of Germany

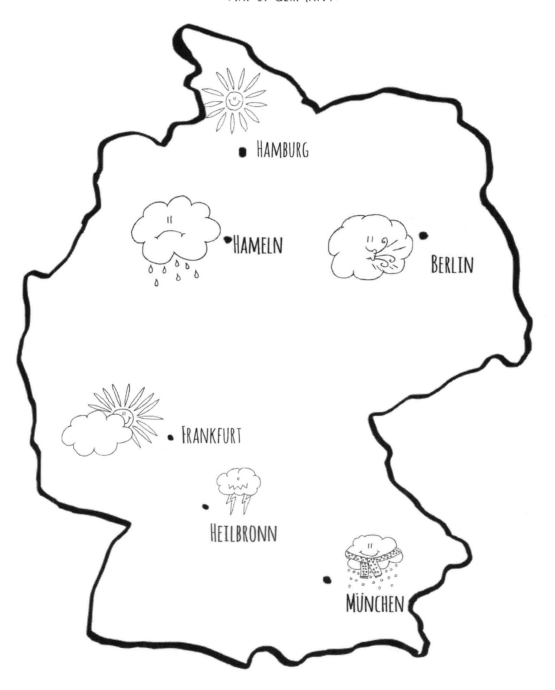

Wie ist das Wetter heute?

B. Schau auf die Karte. Wie ist das Wetter?
Look at the map. What's the weather like?

- Es regnet.	- Es ist windig.	- Die Sonne scheint.
- Es schneit.	- Es gewittert.	

1. Wie ist das Wetter in Hameln?

_____Es regnet_____.

2. Wie ist das Wetter in Heilbronn?

_____.

3. Wie ist das Wetter in München?

_____.

4. Wie ist das Wetter in Hamburg?

_____.

5. Wie ist das Wetter in Berlin?

_____.

6. Wie ist das Wetter in Frankfurt?

_____.

Lese und lerne

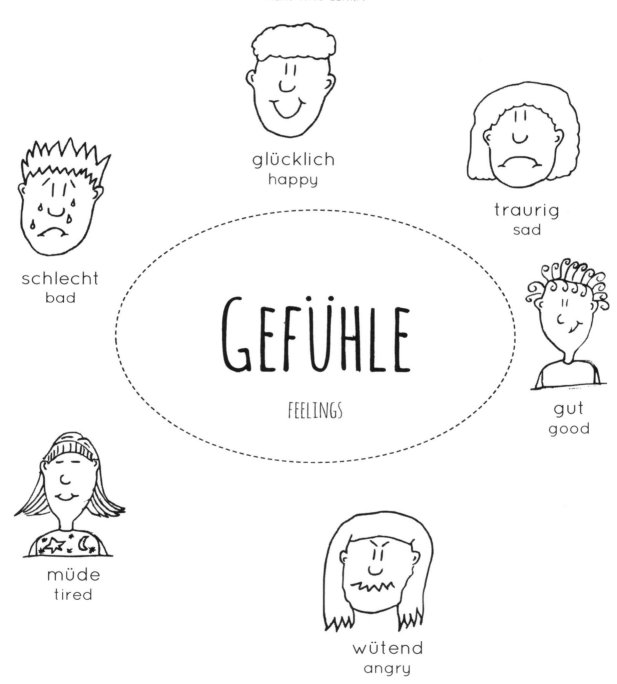

glücklich
happy

traurig
sad

schlecht
bad

Gefühle

feelings

gut
good

müde
tired

wütend
angry

A. Male die Gesichter. Wie fühlen sich die Leute?
Draw the faces. How do the people feel?

glücklich

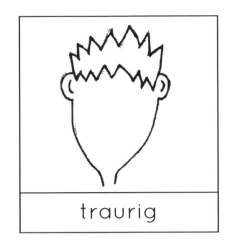

traurig

wütend

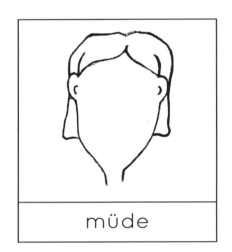

müde

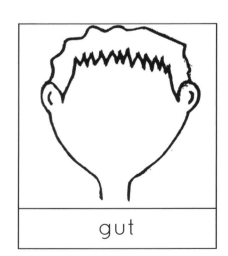

gut

schlecht

BeeGerman.com

B. Beende die Sätze.
Finish the sentences.

gut	müde
schlecht	traurig
wütend	glücklich

1.

   Ich bin TRAURIG.
   I'm sad.

2.

   Mir geht es _____

3.

   Ich bin _____

4.

   Mir geht es _____

5.

   Ich bin _____

6.

   Ich bin _____

Lese und Lerne

der Schal
the scarf

der Rock
the skirt

Die kurze
Hose

das T-Shirt
the t-shirt

der Pullover
the pullover

die
Socken
the socks

Kleidung

clothes

die Mütze
the woollen hat

der Schuh
the shoe

das Kleid
the dress

die Hose
the trousers

die Jacke
the jacket

DIE KLEIDUNG

THE CLOTHES

A. Male die richtigen Kleidungstücke an.
Colour in the correct pieces of clothing.

1. Die Jacke ist blau.
2. Die Hose ist braun.
3. Der Schal ist bunt.
4. Der Schuh ist schwarz.
5. Die Mütze ist gelb.
6. Das Kleid ist rot.
7. Die kurze Hose ist grau.
8. Die Socken sind bunt.
9. Der Rock ist grün.
10. Das T-Shirt ist pink.
11. Der Pullover ist orange.

BeeGerman.com

Lese und Lerne

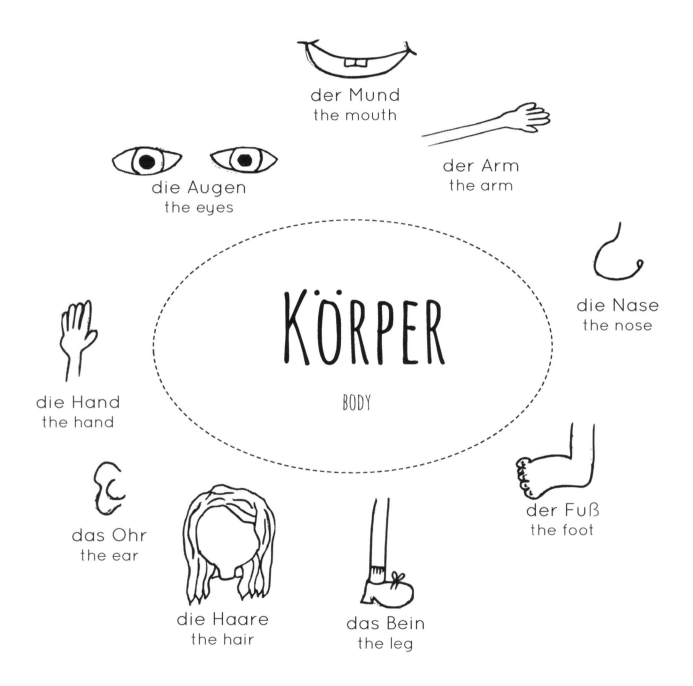

der Mund
the mouth

der Arm
the arm

die Augen
the eyes

die Nase
the nose

Körper

BODY

die Hand
the hand

der Fuß
the foot

das Ohr
the ear

die Haare
the hair

das Bein
the leg

Der Körper

The body

A. Ordne die Wörter zu.
Match the words.

das Ohr	der Arm
die Augen	das Bein
der Mund	die Nase
die Hand	die Haare
der Fuß	

DIE HAARE

B. Wie heißen die Körperteile? Schreibe in den Kasten.
What are the parts of the body called? Write in the box.

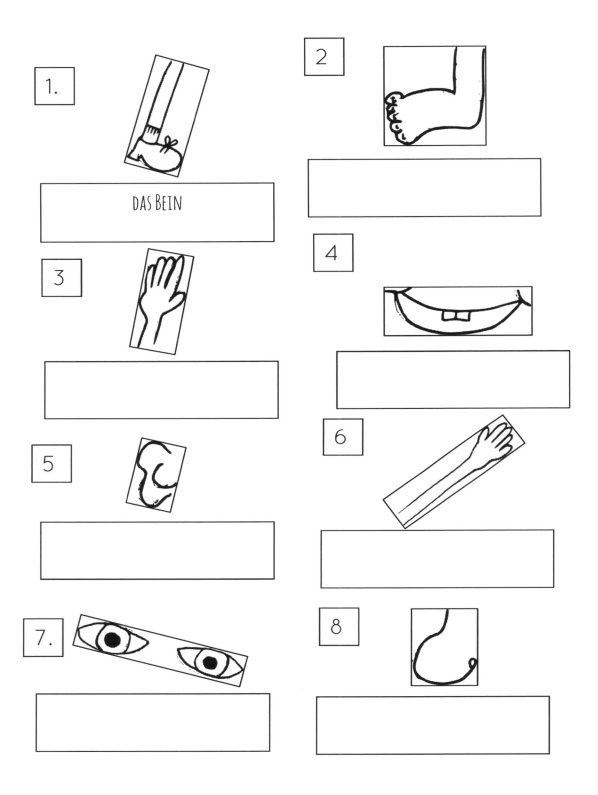

1.

DAS BEIN

2

3

4

5

6

7.

8

BeeGerman.com

Lese und Lerne

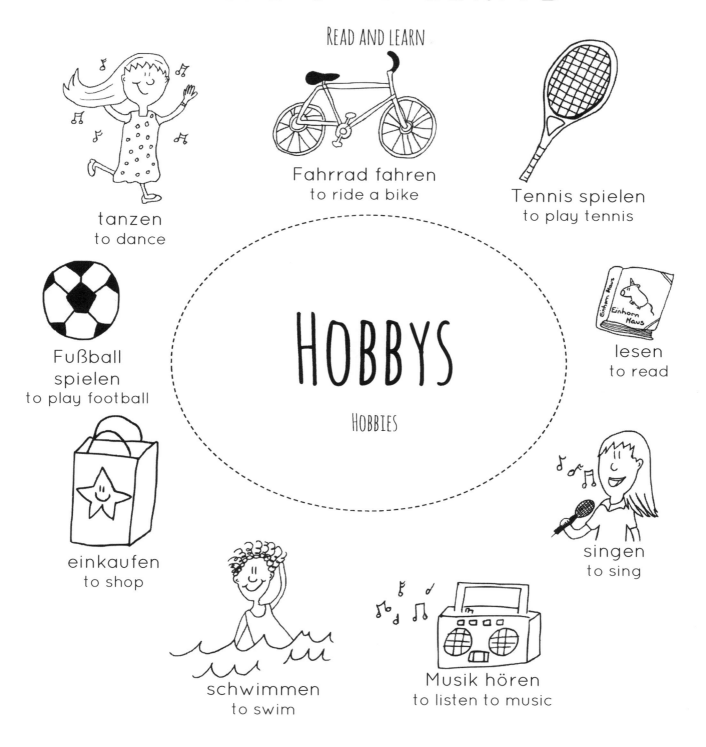

tanzen
to dance

Fahrrad fahren
to ride a bike

Tennis spielen
to play tennis

Fußball
spielen
to play football

HOBBYS

Hobbies

lesen
to read

einkaufen
to shop

singen
to sing

schwimmen
to swim

Musik hören
to listen to music

41

WAS SIND DEINE HOBBYS?

WHAT ARE YOUR HOBBIES?

A. Schreibe die passende Zahl in den Kreis.
Write the correct number in the circle.

1. singen

2. lesen

3. Fußball spielen

4. tanzen

5. einkaufen

6. Musik hören

7. schwimmen

8. Fahrrad fahren

9. Tennis spielen

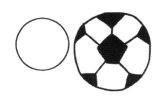

B. Schreibe die richtigen Verbformen in die Lücken.
Write the correct verb forms in the gaps.

Singen	Fahrrad fahren	Tanzen
Fußball spielen	Tennis spielen	
Lesen	Einkaufen	
Schwimmen	Musik hören	

1. Annas Hobby ist SINGEN.
Anna's Hobby is singing.

2. Axels Hobby ist _____.

3. Sabrinas Hobby ist _____.

4. Pauls Hobby ist _____.

5. Heidis Hobby ist _____.

6. Emmas Hobbys sind _____ und

_____.

7. Andreas Hobbys sind _____ und

_____.

BeeGerman.com

STECKBRIEFE

PROFILES

C. Lese die folgenden Steckbriefe. Schreibe dann deinen eigenen Steckbrief und male dein Gesicht.
Read the following profiles. Then write your own profile and draw your face.

- **WIE HEISST DU?**

Mein Name ist Hans Hummel.

- **WIE ALT BIST DU?**

Ich bin 8 Jahre alt.

- **WIE GEHT ES DIR?**

Mir geht es gut, danke.

- **WAS SIND DEINE HOBBYS?**

Meine Hobbys sind Schwimmen und Lesen.

- **WIE HEISST DU?**

Ich heiße Anna Blume.

- **WIE ALT BIST DU?**

Ich bin 7 Jahre alt.

- **WIE GEHT ES DIR?**

Mir geht es super, danke.

- **WAS SIND DEINE HOBBYS?**

Lesen und Fahrrad fahren.

Das bin ich

That's me

Wie heißt du?

_____.

Wie alt bist du?

_____.

Wie geht es dir?

_____.

Was sind deine Hobbys?

_____.

LÖSUNGEN
ANSWERS

Wichtige Wörter/ Sätze
B. p.7
Guten Tag – Good day
Hallo - Hello
Bitte - Please
Guten Morgen - Good mornir
Guten Abend- Good evening
Auf Wiedersehen - Goodbye
Tschüss - Bye
Danke - Thank you
Gute Nacht - Goodnight

C. p.8
Wie geht es dir? - How are you?
Mir geht es gut, danke. - I'm fine, thank you.
Wie heißt du? - What's your name?
Mein Name ist ... - My name is...
Mir geht es schlecht. - I'm unwell.
Ich heiße... - My name is...

Ich und du
A. p.13
ich- I
du - you
er - he
sie - she
es - it
wir - we
ihr - you
sie - they

Wie alt bist du?
D. p. 18
Katrin ist acht Jahre alt.
Anton ist zehn Jahre alt.
Petra ist sechs Jahre alt.
Annika ist sieben Jahre alt.

Farben
B. p. 21
rot - red
pink - pink
braun - brown
schwarz - black
bunt - colourful
grün - green
lila - purple
orange - orange
weiß - white
grau - grey
gelb - yellow
blau - blue

Ich mag...
C. p.22
2. Ja, ich mag Äpfel./ Nein, ich mag keine Äpfel.
3. Ja, ich mag Karotten./ Nein, ich mag keine Karotten.
4. Ja, ich mag Tomaten./ Nein, ich mag keine Tomaten.
5. Ja, ich mag Bananen./ Nein, ich mag keine Bananen.
6. Ja, ich mag Zitronen./ Nein, ich mag keine Zitronen.
7. Ja, ich mag Orangen./ Nein, ich mag keine Orangen.

Wochentage
A. p.23
Montag, Dienstag, Mittwoch, Donnerstag, Freitag, Samstag, Sonntag.

46

Tiere
B. p.26
2. Das ist ein Igel.
3. Das ist ein Hund.
4. Das ist ein Hase.
5. Das ist eine Biene.
6. Das ist eine Ente.
7. Das ist eine Maus.
8. Das ist ein Pferd.
9. Das ist ein Vogel.

Das Wetter
A. p.30
1. der Regen - Es regnet.
2. der Wind - Es ist windig.
3. die Sonne - Die Sonne scheint.
4. die Wolke - Es ist wolkig.
5. der Schnee - Es schneit.
6. Das Gewitter - Es gewittert.

Wie ist das Wetter heute?
B. p.32
2. Es gewittert in Heilbronn.
3. Es schneit in München.
4. Die Sonne scheint in Hambu
5. Es ist windig in Berlin.
6. Es ist wolkig in Frankfurt.

Gefühle
B. p.35
2. Mir geht es gut.
3. Ich bin glücklich.
4. Mir geht es schlecht.
5. Ich bin müde.
6. Ich bin wütend.

Körper
B. p.40
1. das Bein
2. der Fuß
3. die Hand
4. der Mund
5. das Ohr
6. der Arm
7. die Augen
8. die Nase

BIS BALD!
SEE YOU SOON!

Hobbys
B. p.43
2. Axels Hobby ist Fußball spielen.
3. Sabrinas Hobby ist Musik hören.
4. Pauls Hobby ist Fahrrad fahren.
5. Heidis Hobby ist Tennis spielen.
6. Emmas Hobbys sind Lesen und Einkaufen.
7. Andreas Hobbys sind Schwimmen und Tanzen.

BeeGerman.com

Printed in Great Britain
by Amazon